TIP-OFF BASKETBALL

POINT GUARD

By Jason Glaser

Must Read!

Gareth Stevens
Publishing

Please visit our Web site, www.garethstevens.com. For a free color catalog of all our high-quality books, call toll free 1-800-542-2595 or fax 1-877-542-2596.

Library of Congress Cataloging-in-Publication Data

Glaser, Jason.
 Point guard / Jason Glaser.
   p. cm. — (Tip-off: Basketball)
 Includes index.
 ISBN 978-1-4339-3975-4 (pbk.)
 ISBN 978-1-4339-3976-1 (6-pack)
 ISBN 978-1-4339-3974-7 (library binding)
 1. Basketball—Juvenile literature. I. Title.
 GV885.1.G58 2011
 796.323—dc22

                              2010008166

First Edition

Published in 2011 by
Gareth Stevens Publishing
111 East 14th Street, Suite 349
New York, NY 10003

Copyright © 2011 Gareth Stevens Publishing

Designer: Michael J. Flynn
Editor: Greg Roza

Gareth Stevens Publishing would like to thank consultant Stephen Hayn, men's basketball coach at Dowling College, for his guidance in writing this book.

Photo credits: Cover, p. 1 Christian Petersen/Getty Images; cover, back cover, pp. 2–3, 5, 7, 11–13, 17, 21, 26, 31, 35, 41, 44–48 (basketball court background on all), 7, 11, 15, 25–27, 30, 37–39, 42 (basketball border on all), 8, 40, 42, 43 Shutterstock.com; p. 4 D. Clarke Evans/NBAE/Getty Images; p. 5 Andrew D. Bernstein/NBAE/Getty Images; p. 6 Chicago History Museum/Hulton Archive/Getty Images; pp. 9, 38 Jonathan Daniel/Getty Images; p. 10 Hulton Archive/Getty Images; p. 11 Dick Raphael/NBAE/Getty Images; p. 12 Wen Roberts/NBAE/Getty Images; p. 13 NBA Photos/NBAE/Getty Images; p. 14 Ken Levine/Getty Images; pp. 15, 27 Doug Pensinger/Getty Images; p. 16 Cameron Browne/NBAE/Getty Images; p. 17 Ezra Shaw/Getty Images; p. 18 Noah Graham/NBAE/Getty Images; pp. 19, 35 Kevin C. Cox/Getty Images; p. 20 Jim McIsaac/Getty Images; p. 21 Streeter Lecka/Getty Images; p. 22 Al Bello/Getty Images; p. 23 David Liam Kyle/NBAE/Getty Images; pp. 24, 29 David Sherman/NBAE/Getty Images; p. 25 Greg Nelson/Sports Illustrated/Getty Images; p. 26 Gary Dineen/NBAE/Getty Images; p. 28 Glenn James/NBAE/Getty Images; p. 30 Stan Honda/AFP/Getty Images; p. 31 Rocky Widner/NBAE/Getty Images; p. 32 Brian Bahr/Getty Images; p. 33 ChinaFotoPress/Getty Images; pp. 34, 39 Chris Graythen/Getty Images; p. 36 Jesse D. Garrabrant/NBAE/Getty Images; p. 37 Garrett Ellwood/NBAE/Getty Images; p. 41 Hill Street Studios/Blend Images/Getty Images; p. 44 Lisa Blumenfeld/Getty Images; p. 45 Eliot J. Schechter/Getty Images.

Printed in the United States of America

CPSIA compliance information: Batch #CS10GS: For further information contact Gareth Stevens, New York, New York at 1-800-542-2595.

CONTENTS

Boldface words appear in the glossary.

Leaders on the Court

Point guards have the hardest role in basketball. They must direct their teammates and track their **opponents**. Often, a point guard has just seconds to decide whether to pass, shoot, or move. They also have to keep the ball away from the **defense**.

A Playoff Nail-Biter

Game 5 of the 2004 Western Conference Playoffs, between the **NBA**'s San Antonio Spurs and Los Angeles Lakers, was going down to the wire. With just seconds remaining, forward Tim Duncan of the Spurs made a last-second shot over two defenders to put the Spurs ahead 73–72. Actually, it was only a most-of-the-last-second shot. There was still 0.4 second left.

Lakers point guard Gary Payton runs down the court during the 2004 NBA Playoffs.

4

Normally, Lakers point guard Gary Payton would pass to his team's best shooter, Kobe Bryant. With Bryant heavily guarded, fellow guard Derek Fisher broke free. Payton saw Fisher and threw the ball to him. In a flash, Fisher caught it, spun, and launched a perfect shot as the buzzer sounded. The ball swished through the net to give the Lakers the win!

Point guards have to see everything on the court every second to make amazing plays. Keep reading to see what it takes to play this challenging position.

Gary Payton celebrates the Lakers' victory over the Spurs in Game 5 of the 2004 Western Conference Playoffs.

Basketball was played differently when it was invented in 1891. Players couldn't move with the ball. Teammates ran around to get open for passes. Teams passed until someone near the basket could score.

Dropping the Ball

Early teams had nine players: three forwards, three centers, and three guards. By 1900, most teams had five players. Since players couldn't move with the ball, they began "dropping" it and moving after it. **Dribbling**, as the move was called, was added to the game.

This picture, taken around 1905, shows an early basketball game played at a YMCA in Evanston, Illinois.

Cross the Line

Good ball-handling skills can control the speed of the game. Early teams that wanted to keep the lead often moved the ball up and down the court endlessly. The other team had to chase the ball everywhere hoping to steal it. In 1932, basketball leagues added a line at midcourt. Once the **offense** passed the ball over this line, it had to stay across. Shortly after, officials added a rule giving teams only 10 seconds to bring the ball across.

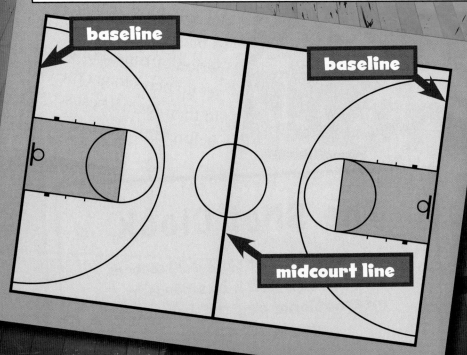

baseline

baseline

midcourt line

A modern NBA court is 94 feet (28.7 m) long. The midcourt line is 47 feet (14.3 m) away from both baselines.

7

shot clock

Even with midcourt lines, good teams could still slow the game down. This was boring to watch. Leagues then added a countdown timer, called the shot clock. If the offense didn't shoot before the clock reached zero, the other team got the ball. Now teams had to make shots in a short period of time. Point guards set up plays to get the ball to their team's best scorers before time ran out.

The Shot Clock

In the NBA, the shot clock is 24 seconds long. In college, it is 35 seconds. In **international** play, the shot clock is usually 30 seconds.

Philadelphia 76er Allen Iverson drives toward the basket during a game against the Chicago Bulls in 2003.

Driving to the Hoop

For a long time, a point guard's job was to pass to a teammate who had an open shot. If everything went well, the teammate scored and the point guard got an **assist**. As point guards became better dribblers, many could get past defenders to make a basket. Players like Allen Iverson, who swirled around opponents before scoring up close, changed the way point guards played the position.

Here are a few of the great players of the past who made the point guard position what it is today.

Bob Cousy

Two Hands, No Problem

After breaking his right arm as a teen in 1941, Bob Cousy learned to dribble with his left. He confused defenses by moving the ball between his hands with ease. Cousy's fast hands **dished** the ball to Boston Celtic teammates the moment they were open. With his great play-making skills and perfect passing, Cousy led the league in assists for 8 straight years in the 1950s.

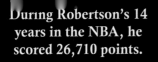

During Robertson's 14 years in the NBA, he scored 26,710 points.

The Big O

Point guards are often the smallest players on the team. Oscar Robertson was among the biggest. He was 6 feet 5 inches (196 cm) tall. The Cincinnati Royals' hometown hero showed greatness right away by becoming **Rookie** of the Year for the 1960–1961 season. "The Big O" was such a great shooter that other teams purposely **fouled** him to keep him from scoring. During the 1963–1964 season, he led the league in assists and points from **free throws**!

"Pistol" Pete Maravich makes a jump shot over the great Wilt Chamberlain.

Pistol Pete

The Atlanta Hawks' Pete Maravich was a scoring point guard. In college during the late 1960s, Maravich set almost every scoring record in **NCAA** history. Amazingly, he did this before the three-point shot was added to basketball. He was named to the Basketball Hall of Fame at the age of 39—one of the youngest players ever honored.

The Robber

Teammates called Walt Frazier "Clyde" after Clyde Barrow, a famous bank robber. Walt was a thief, too. He stole the ball from opponents. His skills on defense as a New York Knick earned him a spot on the NBA All-Defensive First Team for the 1968–1969 season. He won that honor—given to the best defensive players—the following 6 years, too.

During the 1972–1973 season, "Tiny" Archibald led the NBA in minutes played, baskets made, free throws, assists, and points.

Tiny Plays Big

Someone who is 6 feet 1 inch (185 cm) tall may seem tall to you, but that's short in basketball. Yet Nathaniel "Tiny" Archibald came up big on offense. During the 1972–1973 season, Archibald became the only player in history to lead the NBA in both points and assists. Later, he helped the Boston Celtics lead the league in victories for 3 years and win the 1981 NBA Championship.

13

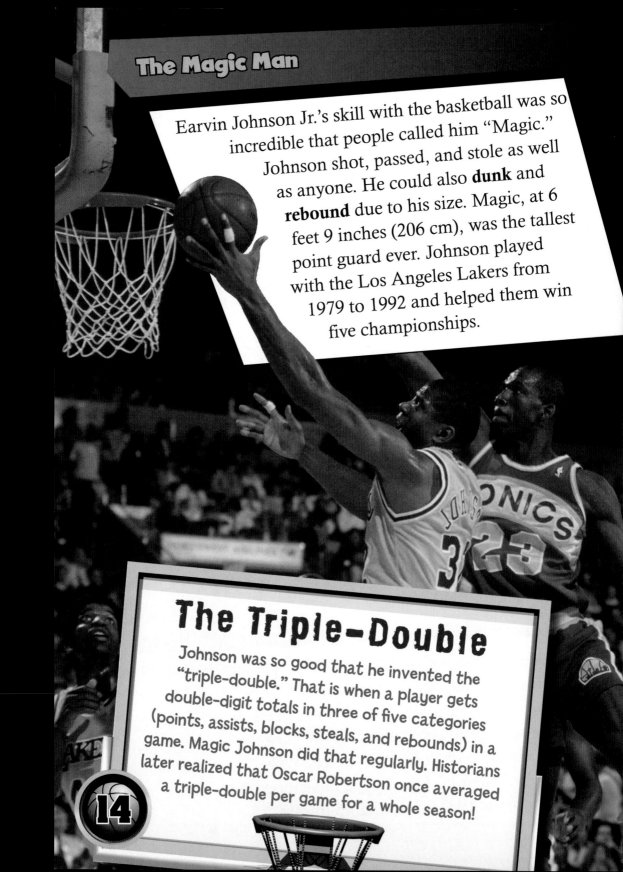

Earvin Johnson Jr.'s skill with the basketball was so incredible that people called him "Magic." Johnson shot, passed, and stole as well as anyone. He could also **dunk** and **rebound** due to his size. Magic, at 6 feet 9 inches (206 cm), was the tallest point guard ever. Johnson played with the Los Angeles Lakers from 1979 to 1992 and helped them win five championships.

The Triple-Double

Johnson was so good that he invented the "triple-double." That is when a player gets double-digit totals in three of five categories (points, assists, blocks, steals, and rebounds) in a game. Magic Johnson did that regularly. Historians later realized that Oscar Robertson once averaged a triple-double per game for a whole season!

John Stockton

John Stockton of the Utah Jazz was a wizard at both offense and defense. Between 1984 and 2003, Stockton racked up 15,806 assists and 3,265 steals—more than anyone in NBA history for each. Stockton and the Jazz never won the NBA Championship, but the Jazz made it to the playoffs every year Stockton played. They made it to the championship series in 1997 and 1998.

John Stockton led the NBA in assists for 9 straight seasons in the 1980s and 1990s.

15

How to Play Point Guard

Playing point guard takes a sharp mind, steady hands, and quick reflexes. Here's a close look at what makes a good point guard.

The Coach on the Court

As team leader, the point guard usually takes the ball first and calls plays to his teammates. Depending on the play, a teammate might break for the basket or **screen** an opponent to free a good shooter. If the point guard calls the right play, his team has a good chance to score a basket.

Point guard Andre Miller of the Portland Trail Blazers sets up a play.

The Mental Checklist

The point guard sets the pace of the play. If his team likes to make quick plays, he might rush with the ball. If the team has a big lead or needs the right play against a good defense, he might dribble slowly into position. Before passing or shooting, a point guard must consider the strength and position of the defense, the time left on the shot and game clocks, and his teammates' abilities.

Chris Paul of the New Orleans Hornets is one of the best point guards in the NBA. He's a quick decision-maker.

On Offense

Point guards have to make choices quickly. The following plays show ways point guards can help put points on the board.

Have a Hot Hand

If the point guard gets the chance, he might try to score. Since the point guard is usually a smaller player, taller defenders can often block long-range shots. The point guard could call for a **pick** to get open for a shot. If the point guard is a great dribbler, he might be able to get past the defenders for a closer shot at the basket.

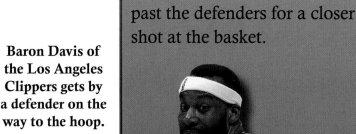

Baron Davis of the Los Angeles Clippers gets by a defender on the way to the hoop.

Miami 67 F Team Foul

Jamal Crawford of the Atlanta Hawks sets up the give and go.

Give and Go

The defense expects point guards to pass. Once the point guard passes, defenders might go after the player receiving the ball. If the point guard moves to the basket right after passing, he might get open. The teammate can then quickly pass the ball back to the point guard, who can make an easy basket.

Knowing that the point guard starts with the ball, one defender is often close by. A point guard may have a teammate set a pick to keep the defender from following him. This frees the point guard to take a shot. If defenders scramble to cover the point guard, the pick setter can often get free. With a quick pass from the point guard, the teammate scores. The pick and roll creates situations in which height mismatches can result in baskets, too.

Let's Get Rolling

Point guard Steve Nash and Amar'e Stoudemire of the Phoenix Suns work the pick and roll perfectly. The big Stoudemire sets the pick for a moving Nash. Then, the defender must choose to follow Nash or guard Stoudemire. In the confusion, Nash or Stoudemire often finds a way to get the ball into the basket.

If the team on defense steals the ball or grabs a rebound, they quickly go on offense. They may have a chance to outrun the other team back across the court. If the point guard doesn't get the steal, he should be open to receive the ball on the run. During a fast break, the point guard may reach the basket before his opponents and score. He may also pass the ball so that an unguarded teammate can score.

Charlotte Bobcats point guard Raymond Fenton scores an easy basket after a fast break.

Point Guards on Defense

On defense, a point guard usually guards the other team's point guard and prevents him from scoring. One way to do this is to steal the ball. If the opponent is distracted, the point guard can grab or hit the dribbled ball. He might even swat it out of the opponent's hands. If the point guard thinks the other player will pass, he needs to cut off the passing lane so the ball can't get by.

Two point guards go at it one-on-one! Deron Williams of the Utah Jazz defends against Devin Harris of the New Jersey Nets.

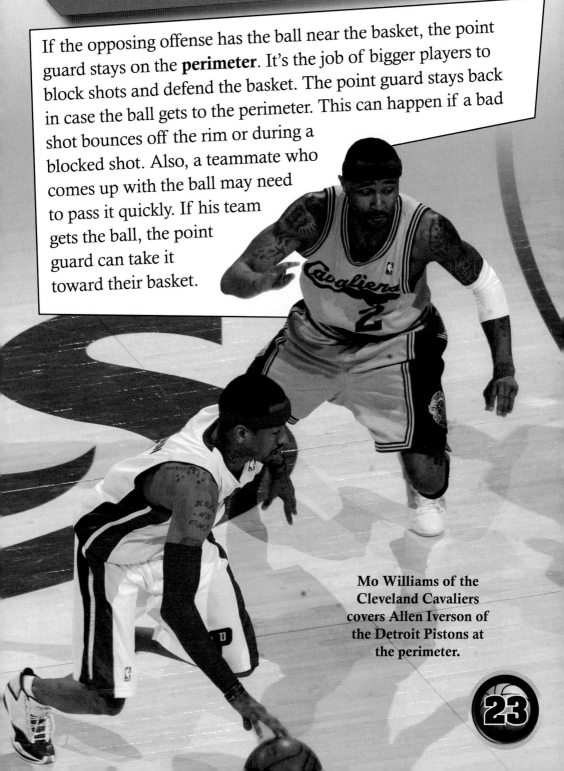

If the opposing offense has the ball near the basket, the point guard stays on the **perimeter**. It's the job of bigger players to block shots and defend the basket. The point guard stays back in case the ball gets to the perimeter. This can happen if a bad shot bounces off the rim or during a blocked shot. Also, a teammate who comes up with the ball may need to pass it quickly. If his team gets the ball, the point guard can take it toward their basket.

Mo Williams of the Cleveland Cavaliers covers Allen Iverson of the Detroit Pistons at the perimeter.

Key Skills

A point guard must be ready for anything. Here are some skills point guards need to help their team.

People Skills

The point guard has to lead by example. He must be confident and work hard. A point guard should never bad-mouth another player or the coach. He must keep problems from causing distractions and keep his teammates' minds on the game.

The Minnesota Timberwolves point guard Jonny Flynn is known as a great leader and communicator on the court.

Court Vision

A point guard has to be able to see everything and make decisions quickly. If defenders are tired or out of position, he calls a play to take advantage. If a play breaks down, the point guard must make a change. He may have to find an open player and get the ball to him fast. On defense, he must see opponents setting screens and warn his team.

Many consider Jason Kidd of the Dallas Mavericks the best point guard in basketball today. Here he calls a play while protecting the ball.

Eyes Up!

The point guard's eyes have to be on the action. He must be able to dribble with either hand without watching the ball. This lets him keep the ball away from defenders. Keeping his eyes free means the point guard can see the court to make a good play.

When a point guard doesn't have the ball, he needs to be ready to get it. He stands in a low crouch, ready to spring into motion. His feet form a wide base. If his feet are too close together, he won't be able to make a quick move. On defense, his hands are low so he can attempt to steal the ball.

Toronto Raptor José Calderón prepares to spring into action.

Chauncey Billups of the Denver Nuggets springs into action against the Cleveland Cavaliers.

Always Moving

The point guard moves around a lot. On offense, he has to be able to sprint away from defenders or over to an open spot for a pass. On defense, the point guard can try to stop a break before the ball even gets to the midcourt line. He also runs around the perimeter, defending outside shooters and chasing the ball.

Pass or Fail

A point guard needs to get the ball to his team's scorers to win the game. There are several ways the point guard can pass the ball to a teammate and avoid a turnover.

Two-Handed Chest Pass

The most common pass is the two-handed chest pass. To prepare for a two-handed chest pass, the point guard holds the ball close to his chest with both hands. When a teammate gets open, the point guard fires off the ball with both hands. The teammate catches the quick pass and makes his move.

Jamaal Tinsley of the Memphis Grizzlies makes a two-handed chest pass to a teammate.

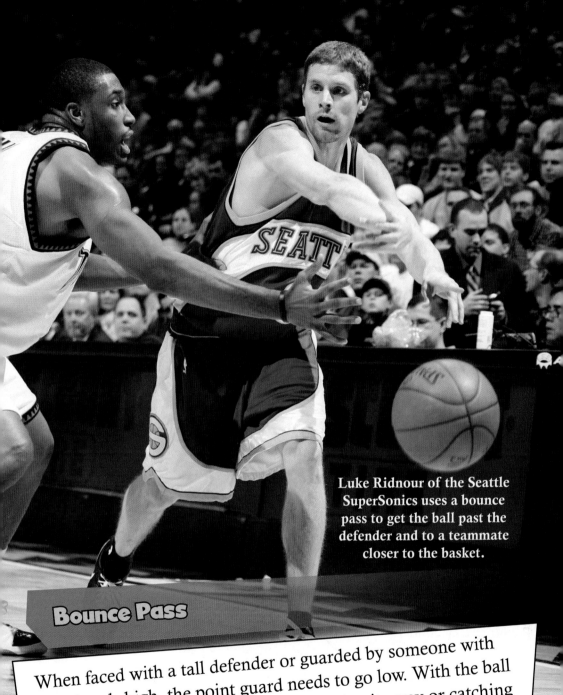

Luke Ridnour of the Seattle SuperSonics uses a bounce pass to get the ball past the defender and to a teammate closer to the basket.

Bounce Pass

When faced with a tall defender or guarded by someone with their hands high, the point guard needs to go low. With the ball low, the defense has a harder time knocking it away or catching it. The point guard throws the ball toward the floor between him and his teammate. The pass bounces off the court and up into the teammate's hands.

29

Overhead Pass

To get the ball to a taller player, or to prevent a defender from sweeping the ball away low, the point guard uses an overhead pass. He brings the ball up above his head with both hands. He puts speed on the ball by snapping his wrists as he throws. The teammate catches the ball up high where he can make a shot on the basket.

Jameer Nelson of the Orlando Magic uses an overhead pass to get the ball to an open teammate.

The Fake-Shot Pass

Defenders will always try to cut off or steal a pass. Many opponents stay close in front of the ball handler to have a better chance of stealing the ball. A point guard can give himself some space for a pass by faking a shot. The defender will often raise his arms or jump to block. The point guard then passes beneath the defender's arms to a teammate.

After a fake shot, Philadelphia 76er Allen Iverson easily dishes the ball to a teammate who is open.

31

Point Guard Points

Every player on the court needs to be able to make a basket, including the point guard. If the defense has to cover a point guard who can shoot, the guard can set up plays for other players.

Shooting on the Move

When driving to the basket, a point guard doesn't always have time to set his feet before shooting. He must be able to cut in as close as possible and then get the ball up to the basket. By using the backboard, the point guard can angle the ball into the basket with a **layup**. Skillful ball handlers sometimes underhand the ball to get it by a blocker's arms, rolling the ball up and off their fingers.

Beno Udrih of the San Antonio Spurs moves in close for a layup.

Stephon Marbury goes for three points! Formerly an NBA superstar, Marbury now plays for the Shanxi Zhongyu Brave Dragons of the Chinese Basketball Association.

Outside Threat

Since the point guard plays away from the basket, the most likely shot for him to make is from the perimeter. Point guards can fool a defender by pretending to move or pass. They then have the chance to put up a jump shot. Good control and a nice, high arc will send the ball swishing through the net.

The Three-Point Shot

The three-point line is an arc 20.5 feet (6.25 m) away from the basket on a basketball court. Jump shots made from behind this line are worth 3 points. Point guards who are good at three-point shots can score a lot of points for their team.

Modern Marvels

Some of the greatest point guards in history are still playing professional basketball. Here are a few who shine at their position.

CP3

Many people consider Chris Paul of the New Orleans Hornets to be the best point guard playing today. He entered the NBA in 2005 and was named Rookie of the Year for the 2005–2006 season. In his first 4 years, he led the league in steals three times and assists twice. His string of 108 games in a row with one or more steals is an NBA record.

Chris Paul is called CP3 because his father, Charles Paul (CP1), and brother, C. J. Paul (CP2), have the same initials!

In Nash-Ville

During the 2004–2005 season, the Phoenix Suns' Steve Nash became just the fifth point guard ever to win the NBA's Most Valuable Player (MVP) award. He then won it again the following year. Nash's **accuracy** as a passer and shooter have made him the league leader in assists and shooting percentage several times.

Steve Nash was born in Johannesburg, South Africa, in 1974. His family moved to Canada when he was 1 year old.

Few people can claim to have changed a sports position the way Allen Iverson has. In the past, point guards rarely charged straight to the basket. However, Iverson has shown how smaller, quicker players can get inside and make a shot, too. Since entering the NBA in 1996, Iverson's ability to drive to the basket has made him one of the all-time leading scorers. In 2005, he once scored 60 points in a single game. He has won the league scoring title three times.

For the 2004–2005 season, Iverson led the NBA in points scored with 2,302.

Chauncey Billups of the Denver Nuggets may not have won many honors, but he has the one that matters most: NBA Champion. In 2004, Chauncey Billups led the Detroit Pistons (his team at the time) to victory over the Los Angeles Lakers and was named Finals MVP. His teammates call Billups "Mr. Big Shot" because of how well he shoots from the perimeter under pressure. Billups's team has made the playoffs every year since 2001.

A familiar sight for Nuggets fans, Chauncey Billups makes a jump shot from the perimeter.

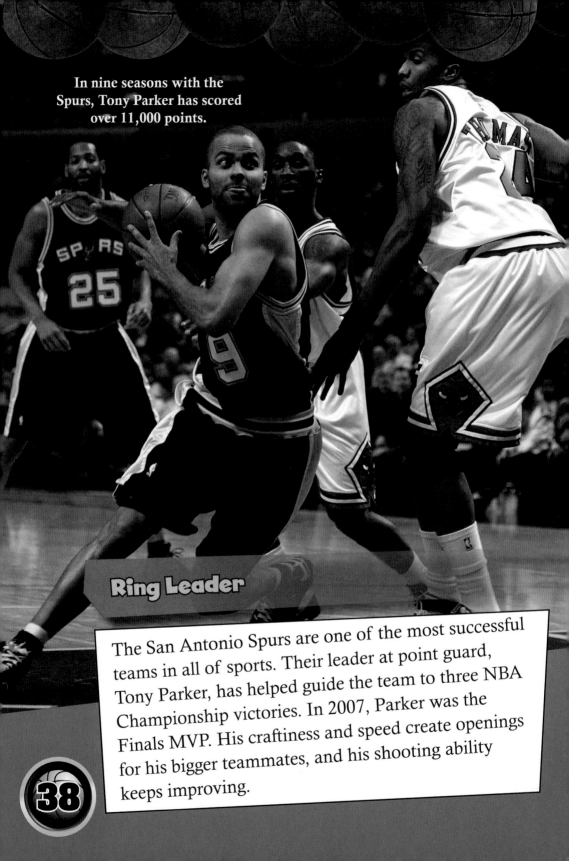

In nine seasons with the Spurs, Tony Parker has scored over 11,000 points.

Ring Leader

The San Antonio Spurs are one of the most successful teams in all of sports. Their leader at point guard, Tony Parker, has helped guide the team to three NBA Championship victories. In 2007, Parker was the Finals MVP. His craftiness and speed create openings for his bigger teammates, and his shooting ability keeps improving.

Basketball is a team sport, but some say Jason Kidd single-handedly turned the New Jersey Nets around. Kidd came into a suffering team and led it on two straight trips to the NBA Finals. Kidd's numbers are incredible. He is the only player in NBA history to earn over 15,000 points, 10,000 assists, and 7,000 rebounds. He has the second-most career assists and the third-most triple-doubles of anyone in history.

Jason Kidd began his career with the Dallas Mavericks in 1994. He played for the Phoenix Suns and the New Jersey Nets. Today, Kidd is back with the Mavericks.

05 Future Star: You!

Want to be a great point guard? Here are some important skills to work on.

Balanced Ball Handling

A good point guard can dribble well with either hand. Try dribbling the length of the court with your **dominant** hand and then back with your other hand. Then repeat while passing the ball back and forth from hand to hand. Practice until you can use either hand at top speed without looking at the ball.

A Burst of Speed!

A point guard needs to be fast. You should practice sprints to make yourself faster and build your **endurance**.

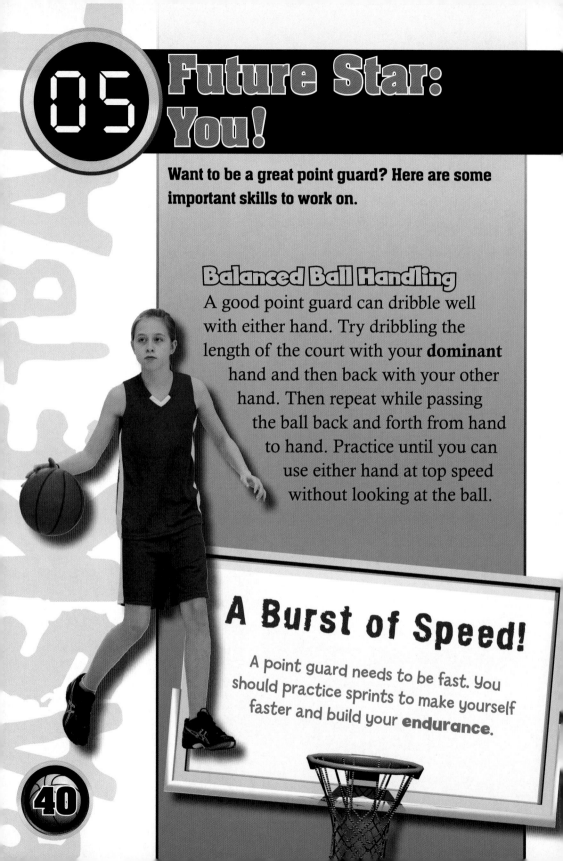

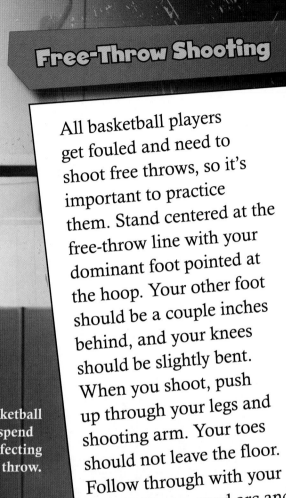

Free-Throw Shooting

All basketball players get fouled and need to shoot free throws, so it's important to practice them. Stand centered at the free-throw line with your dominant foot pointed at the hoop. Your other foot should be a couple inches behind, and your knees should be slightly bent. When you shoot, push up through your legs and shooting arm. Your toes should not leave the floor. Follow through with your hand to put a good arc and spin on your shot.

Some basketball players spend hours perfecting their free throw.

When practicing passes, position your feet shoulder width apart. Step forward when passing to give the ball more speed.

Hit the Target

Have a teammate stand on the court about 12 feet (3.7 m) away with their hands out front. Pass the ball back and forth, starting with two-handed chest passes. Use both hands and try to get the ball right to your friend's open hands. After a while, move to bounce passes. Angle the ball off the floor and into your friend's hands, just as you did with chest passes.

With good defensive skills, a point guard can stop the opponent from scoring and create scoring opportunities for their own team.

Take It Away!

Play one-on-one with another player to practice your defense and steals. Stay low and in front of your opponent, positioned slightly nearer to the dribbling hand. Watch the player's chest and not their feet or hands. This will help you determine which way the player will go. Try to take or knock the ball away without letting your opponent get by you. Use a side-to-side motion to clear the ball. Faking a steal can show you how the other player will react.

Record Book

Who are the best point guards of all time? Here are the top five point guards in several key categories.

Career Assists by a Point Guard:

1. John Stockton **15,806**
2. Jason Kidd (still active) **10,923** (as of 5/3/10)
3. Mark Jackson **10,334**
4. Magic Johnson **10,141**
5. Oscar Robertson **9,887**

Single Season Assists by a Point Guard:

1. John Stockton **1,164** 1990–1991
2. John Stockton **1,134** 1989–1990
3. John Stockton **1,128** 1987–1988
4. John Stockton **1,126** 1991–1992
5. Isiah Thomas **1,123** 1984–1985

Single Game Assists by a Point Guard:

1. Scott Skiles **30** 1990
2. John Stockton **28** 1991
3. John Stockton **27** 1989
4. John Stockton **26** 1988
5. Jason Kidd (still active) **25** 1996
   Kevin Johnson **25** 1994
   Nate McMillan **25** 1987

John Stockton

Career Steals by a Point Guard:

1. John Stockton   **3,265**
2. Gary Payton   **2,445**
3. Maurice Cheeks   **2,310**
4. Jason Kidd (still active)   **2,260**
5. Mookie Blaylock   **2,075**

Single Season Steals by a Point Guard:

1. Don Buse   **346** 1975–1976
2. Don Buse   **281** 1976–1977
3. John Stockton   **263** 1988–1989
4. Slick Watts   **261** 1975–1976
5. John Stockton   **244** 1991–1992

All-Star Game Appearances by Point Guards:

1. Bob Cousy   **13**
2. Magic Johnson   **12**
   Oscar Robertson   **12**
4. Isiah Thomas   **11**
   Allen Iverson (still active)   **11**

accuracy: the ability to avoid mistakes

assist: when a player makes a pass that enables a teammate to score

defense: the team trying to stop the other team from scoring

dish: to make a quick, accurate pass

dominant: the stronger one with more control

dribble: to move around the court while bouncing the ball on the floor

dunk: to throw the basketball into the basket from above the rim

endurance: the ability to handle prolonged physical activity

foul: a penalty called for breaking the rules, usually coming from illegal contact between players

free throw: a chance to shoot for one point after being fouled; the shot is made from a line in front of the basket with no defenders

international: involving two or more countries

layup: a shot made from beneath the basket by bouncing the ball off the backboard and into the net

NBA: National Basketball Association, the men's professional basketball league in the United States; the NBA also includes the Toronto (Canada) Raptors

NCAA: National Collegiate Athletic Association, the organization that oversees sports competition between colleges

offense: the team trying to score

opponent: the person or team you must beat to win a game

perimeter: the area away from the basket and outside the foul circle

pick: when a teammate screens for the player with the ball

rebound: a ball recovered off a missed shot

reflexes: the ability to react quickly

rookie: a person playing his first year in a sport

screen: a play where one player moves to block a defender to give a teammate a chance to get open for a pass

Books

Bowen, Fred. *Full Court Fever.* Atlanta, GA: Peachtree Press, 2009.

Doeden, Matt. *The World's Greatest Basketball Players.* Mankato, MN: Capstone Press, 2010.

Eule, Brian. *Basketball for Fun!* Minneapolis, MN: Compass Point Books, 2003.

Gunderson, Jessica. *Full Court Pressure.* Mankato, MN: Stone Arch Books, 2010.

Hicks, Betty. *Basketball Bats.* New York, NY: Roaring Book Press, 2008.

Mantell, Paul. *Nothin' but Net.* Boston, MA: Little, Brown and Company, 2003.

Schaller, Bob, and Dave Harnish. *The Everything Kids' Basketball Book.* Avon, MA: Adams Media, 2009.

Web Sites

www.hoophall.com
Learn about the history of basketball at the online version of the Naismith Memorial Basketball Hall of Fame. Read the biographies of the greatest basketball players of all time.

www.nba.com
The official Web site of the National Basketball Association has information about teams and players both current and historic. Fans can see video, get news, check scores, and look over game or season statistics.

www.nba.com/kids
The NBA's official Web page for kids lets you play games, join fan clubs for your favorite team, and learn exercises to make you a better basketball player.

www.sikids.com/basketball/nba
The *Sports Illustrated* Web page for kids lets you follow your favorite NBA team. On this site, you'll find scores and news updates about your favorite sport.

About the Author

Jason Glaser is a freelance writer and stay-at-home father living in Mankato, Minnesota. He has written over fifty nonfiction books for children, including books on sports stars like Tim Duncan. When he isn't listening to sports radio or writing, Jason likes to play volleyball and put idealized versions of himself into sports video games.